A Journey of Blessings

Living Life Daily, Through God!

Poems Written By:
Ponethetta Ivy Taylor

Order this book online at www.trafford.com
or email orders@trafford.com

Most Trafford titles are also available at major online book retailers.

Printed in Victoria, BC, Canada.

ISBN: 978-1-4269-2848-2 (sc)
ISBN: 978-1-4269-2849-9 (hc)
ISBN: 978-1-4269-3121-5 (eb)

Library of Congress Control Number: 2010905019

*Our mission is to efficiently provide the world's finest, most comprehensive book publishing
service, enabling every author to experience success. To find out how to publish your book, your
way, and have it available worldwide, visit us online at www.trafford.com*

Trafford rev. 04/27/2010

Trafford
PUBLISHING® www.trafford.com

North America & international
toll-free: 1 888 232 4444 (USA & Canada)
phone: 250 383 6864 ♦ fax: 812 355 4082

Dear. God,

I would like to Thank You once again for allowing me such a Blessed opportunity.

Sincerely,
Ponethetta Ivy Taylor

Dedication

To my wonderful parents, Leon and Joan Taylor, Love You Much!

My Brothers, Oliver and Boo(Leon)

My Son, Quadé

My Sister-in-laws: Fran and Dana

My Nephews: Brandon, Jordan, Troy, Lateef, and Aamir

My Nieces: Ashleigh, Arianna, and Aaliyah

Mama Essie, Mama Georgia, Mama Sinclair, and Miss Lillie

My Sister-Friends: Renee, Serene, Ursula, Jerelyn, and Denise

My host of Aunts, Uncle, Cousins, and Family-Friends

Love You All Dearly!

"Come Along With Me, Through This Journey of Blessings!"

Dear. Family-Friends,

I would like to take this opportunity to share with you as God shares with me. Life is a journey as we move from one thing to another. Just keep your focus on Him and He will see you out. Read these poems at your leisure. Take time to write and reflect. I know you will realize how much you are Blessed! Spread the word, tell all, and share your testimony. I hope too one day I will be reading your story.

Sincerely Written,
Pon

A Journey of Blessings will allow you to connect, relate, realize make note and become aware of God's Goodness. I am Blessed to share such an opportunity and be a part of this plan, His plan! As you read the many poems in this book, take the time to see how the words, lines, and/or phrases relate to you. I hope through your reading, you stay connected with His Goodness!

On this Journey of Blessings, a place is provided after each poem for you to write your thoughts. Reflect as needed. Write about the poem and what it means to "You!" We are all faced with challenging issues. However, we experience similar outcomes.... It is important we are able to express our Gratefulness and show Appreciation. This will remind ourselves why we are able and continue to remain wholesome.

In the back of the book, there is a daily journal log. As you read the various poems, there may be that one poem which may have an impact or influence on your life or just the right words, at the right time. You may also need encouragement to help support or ease your mind. Write on a daily basis or whenever you feel the need. However, please be mindful, without God's Grace and Mercy, Where would you be?

Somehow!

June 1990 Springfield Gardens High School,
I walked across the stage.
Off to another level in my life,
the beginning of a new page.
My mind was set to work in the medical field,
as a Pediatrician.
Somehow was refocused into,
a much more needed position.
In continuing my studies I graduated,
Associates Degree, Education-Liberal Arts.
Never knew as a Paraprofessional,
NYC is where I would start.
Somehow through this experience,
moving on to earn a Bachelor of Arts Degree.
Undergrad, Queens College,
major in Sociology and Psychology.
There is where I still had in mind,
to deal with issues in health.
Somehow orders were there, to make it clear,
I was needed somewhere else.
Could only dream of the day,
my name was called, a Master of Science Degree.
Mercy College, Bronx, New York,
in Secondary Education and Students with Disabilities.
By this time became a teacher,

instructing, encouraging, as well as I was motivated.

Somehow began to realize I was a tool,

used in school, for God has created.

To think again, the thought of me to return for another,

as Renee delivered this message.

Master of Science Degree in School Supervision and Administration,

as I dried my eyes, through this session.

After nine years in NYC's public schools,

plans once again rearranged.

Somehow packed my belongings, relocated,

to a whole new place, feeling strange.

However, never did I fear because,

He has not ever failed me yet.

Just a continuation to be used as a tool,

in Virginia, is where I set.

No differences, nor better than,

because all of our youth need guided direction.

Somehow! Somehow! I now know,

this was done by His many Blessings.

So every day as I continue to pray,

Cause this task was aligned for me.

Within His care and rested peace,

traveling a Blessed Journey.

Somehow!

Only through God!

Contents

Everyday Praises

7 Days A Week!

On Monday

I bowed my head and gave God Thanks

Tuesday

Was very similar to add, what Joy He brings

Wednesday

I remained the same as I praised Him loud and clear

Thursday

Came, so grateful and I was filled with many tears

Friday

I lifted my hands high in wanting to touch

On Saturday

I recognized how He loves me so much

Sunday

Is no different because I praise Him everyday

As He prepares me for another week,

Thank You God for making a way!

Everyday Praises _____

_____
_____
_____
_____
_____
_____
_____
_____
_____
_____
_____
_____
_____
_____
_____
_____
_____
_____
_____
_____
_____
_____
_____
_____
_____
_____
_____
_____
_____
_____
_____
_____
_____
_____
_____
_____

Reflect Reflect

Reflect Reflect
Oh how I never forget

God has brought me a mighty long way
And my journey is not done yet.

All His plans reveal
As I continue to Praise His wonderful name

Abundantly, He Blesses me
As well as you and this will never change.

So Reflect Reflect and Never forget

God has brought us a mighty long way
And our journey is not done yet.

Oh how He keeps thee everyday
So continue to pray

He is so Awesome
So stay out of His way.

God is in control
and His plans will bring you through

Reflect Reflect for the good things
and the challenging times too.

Reflect Reflect!

Reflect Reflect _____

_____
_____
_____
_____
_____
_____
_____
_____
_____
_____
_____
_____
_____
_____
_____
_____
_____
_____
_____
_____
_____
_____
_____
_____
_____
_____
_____
_____
_____
_____
_____
_____
_____

I Pray

My mind is made up
And only heaven knows

So many thoughts in my head
When I pray to stop, drop, and flow.

If I had to put a time
As to how long this should last

Yester-years, would be right here
And more time would truly pass.

There's so much to pray about
Sometimes I don't know where to begin

For each I do, so here's to you
Cause really there is no end.

I Pray _____

_____

_____

_____

_____

_____

_____

_____

_____

_____

_____

_____

_____

_____

_____

_____

_____

_____

_____

_____

_____

_____

_____

_____

_____

_____

_____

_____

_____

_____

_____

_____

_____

_____

_____

Open Eyes!

I'm turned upside down

Things are all in a mess,

As I look at my life

I still have no less.

Confused and unstable to do

As I wish,

Unclear frame of mind

The thoughts still exist.

I feel I have nothing

But something is there,

Although I'm turned upside down

Now it's all clear.

I was tossed into frenzy

Just to realize,

God sure has a way to really open my eyes.

Open Eyes!_____

_____
_____
_____
_____
_____
_____
_____
_____
_____
_____
_____
_____
_____
_____
_____
_____
_____
_____
_____
_____
_____
_____
_____
_____
_____
_____
_____
_____
_____
_____
_____
_____
_____
_____
_____
_____
_____
_____
_____

Ahead of Time

Ahead of time, I say Thank You!

I feel Goodness moving inside

Ahead of time, I say Thank You!

My tears well up and down my face,

They continue to slide.

Ahead of time, I say Thank You!

I know I could never repay

Ahead of time, I say Thank You!

I make sure to say it each and every day.

Ahead of time, I say Thank You!

Cause do I really deserve?

Ahead of time, I say Thank You!

As I utter over and over these words,

Thank You! Thank You!

Thank You!

Ahead of Time _____

_____
_____
_____
_____
_____
_____
_____
_____
_____
_____
_____
_____
_____
_____
_____
_____
_____
_____
_____
_____
_____
_____
_____
_____
_____
_____
_____
_____
_____
_____
_____
_____
_____

Too Blessed

I went to count my Blessings
And Oh what a job

I tried to put them in a sack
And it was very hard.

I grabbed one and then another came
So I had to move real fast

The Blessings just kept falling
Didn't know how long this would last.

Even as I write
And even as I breathe

Too many Blessings surrounding,
Can't believe it's all for me.
One may question,
What have I done to obtain such a pile?

If you understood, how God is so good,
You too would want to Smile!

Too Blessed _____

_____
_____
_____
_____
_____
_____
_____
_____
_____
_____
_____
_____
_____
_____
_____
_____
_____
_____
_____
_____
_____
_____
_____
_____
_____
_____
_____
_____
_____
_____
_____
_____
_____
_____
_____

A Wall

Sometimes there is a wall,
In which you feel you cannot climb.

A block in your way,
Just pushing you further behind.

The thought of crawling over,
Is not going to do.

Feeling forced to proceed
But nothing works for you.

Your back you have turned,
Head down as you sob,

Just the very thought of this blockage,
Seems very hard.
A challenge as you struggle
To get through this ordeal,

Understand the wall will not fall,
Until God is revealed.

A Wall _____

An Everlasting Praise!

I need this time to Thank Him,
Pardon me as I step into my zone.

God has kept me wholesome,
And still has not left me alone.

Speak to Him on your time,
But I need to Praise Him now.

Excuse Me! Once again, not to ignore,
This may take a while.

I will talk to you later,
I hope you can understand.

See when I praise Him for me,
I pray for you, we are all a part of His plan.

I don't need to wait until Sunday,
It's a daily thing I do,

If it was not for His Goodness and Mercy,
I would not be speaking to you.

Like selfishly I praise,
To give all Worship and Glory.

Thanks for your time, while listening to,
My non ending, Grateful story.

An Everlasting Praise _____

_____
_____
_____
_____
_____
_____
_____
_____
_____
_____
_____
_____
_____
_____
_____
_____
_____
_____
_____
_____
_____
_____
_____
_____
_____
_____
_____
_____
_____
_____
_____
_____
_____
_____

Regardless of.................

Regardless of, He Blesses any day,

As many don't deserve, He will pave our way.

Catch us when we fall so low to the ground,

Place a smile on our faces, instead or a frown.

Regardless of, He Blesses every day,

God's time is valuable; we would be broke, if we had to pay.

No one could ever do things for us with such love and care,

Twenty-four, seven, by our side and truly sincere.

Regardless of, He Blesses abundantly,

Filling our basket of opportunities.

However, it's up to us, to obey His commands,

As we comfortably sit in the palm of His hands.

Regardless Of......................!

Regardless Of....................._____

_____
_____
_____
_____
_____
_____
_____
_____
_____
_____
_____
_____
_____
_____
_____
_____
_____
_____
_____
_____
_____
_____
_____
_____
_____
_____
_____
_____
_____
_____
_____
_____
_____
_____
_____

Letting Go!

Let go of yesterday
Begin a new chapter.

Forget and leave behind the old
But bring on the laughter.

For only when you release
All that baggage once claimed.

Replace with the love of God
And a new outlook you have gained.

You will be able to smile
While others will not understand.

Even if you can't put the words together,
Just simply wave your hands.

However, you need to move on
So you can fill your purpose.
You will realize through God,
It was all worth.......

Letting Go Yesterday!

Letting Go! _____

_____
_____
_____
_____
_____
_____
_____
_____
_____
_____
_____
_____
_____
_____
_____
_____
_____
_____
_____
_____
_____
_____
_____
_____
_____
_____
_____
_____
_____
_____
_____
_____
_____
_____
_____

Accept My Friend

Get Away, Stay Away,
From my soul.

I have a very special friend
And His hand I hold.

He leads me and guides me,
Not to drift astray.

I would not trade Him for the world,
He is the maker of my day.

When you approach my zone,
I feel tense in the air.

However, if you make Him your friend,
I am willing to share.
Believe me when I say,
He is like no one else.

But you have to accept Him in your life,
And see for yourself!

Accept My Friend_____

_____
_____
_____
_____
_____
_____
_____
_____
_____
_____
_____
_____
_____
_____
_____
_____
_____
_____
_____
_____
_____
_____
_____
_____
_____
_____
_____
_____
_____
_____
_____
_____
_____
_____

God Within Me

I Am A Rocket!

I feel like I can fly, through the sky across the ocean to see,

Am I really a rocket? Or Is that God within me?

Climbing the tallest mountain to touch its white peak,

Am I really a rocket? Or Is that God within me?

Soaring to a high level where no bird has ever reached,

Am I really a rocket? Or Is that God within me?

Stretch out like an airplane, flying with no wings,

Am I really a rocket? Or Is that God within me?

Sit like a helicopter while remaining in air on my feet,

Am I really a rocket? Or Is that God within me?

When you have God in heart all limits are obsolete,

Yes, I do feel like a rocket cause God Is Within Me!

God Within Me _____

_____
_____
_____
_____
_____
_____
_____
_____
_____
_____
_____
_____
_____
_____
_____
_____
_____
_____
_____
_____
_____
_____
_____
_____
_____
_____
_____
_____
_____
_____
_____
_____
_____

P is for Purpose

P is the Plan He has for your life,

U is so Unique, created by Him especially right.

R is for the Road in which He has set,

P is for the Pleasure of being so Blessed.

O He is always On time for your every need,

S gives Strength to nurture you, the seed.

E is for Everything so Praise Him every day,

P is for Purpose, Now you are well on your way!

P is for Purpose! _____

_____

_____

_____

_____

_____

_____

_____

_____

_____

_____

_____

_____

_____

_____

_____

_____

_____

_____

_____

_____

_____

_____

_____

_____

_____

_____

_____

_____

_____

_____

_____

_____

_____

_____

_____

_____

_____

What's Stress!

What's stress if you rest?
Through the Goodness of God.

What's stress if you rest?
Whether easy or hard.

What's stress if you rest?
Casting all your concerns as you pray.

What's stress if you rest?
Knowing God will make a way.

What's stress if you rest?
Wait until your seasoned time.

What's stress if you rest?
God's way, guaranteed things will be fine.

What's stress if you rest?
Believe with all your heart.

No Stress, Just the Best,
Which comes from God!

What's Stress?_____

_____

_____

_____

_____

_____

_____

_____

_____

_____

_____

_____

_____

_____

_____

_____

_____

_____

_____

_____

_____

_____

_____

_____

_____

_____

_____

_____

_____

_____

_____

_____

_____

_____

_____

On This Day!

On this day, someone did not breathe like yesterday.

On this day, someone will be unable to see things come their way.

On this day, someone will not hear the Goodness of His work.

On this day, someone does not understand his value and all He is worth.

On this day, someone will have no food to nourish their soul.

On this day, someone will be living outside in the cold.

On this day, someone will not have money to pay their bills.

On this day, someone will treat another wrong, maybe even kill.

On this day, someone will not see any future plans.

On this day, someone will be unable to use both of their hands.

On this day, someone will have no gas in their car to go.

On this day, someone will send a resume and told later no.

On this day, someone will not be able to purchase medical supplies.

On this day, someone's heart is broken due to unfortunate lies.

On this day, someone will have aches and pains having to remain in bed.

On this day someone will believe in God and listen to what He said:

On this day, I have provided for each and every one of your needs.

On this day, I have forgiven each and every, and love you unconditionally.

On this day, I was the same as yesterday and be tomorrow still.

On this day, I have never left your side and I never will!

On This Day!

On This Day! _____

_____
_____
_____
_____
_____
_____
_____
_____
_____
_____
_____
_____
_____
_____
_____
_____
_____
_____
_____
_____
_____
_____
_____
_____
_____
_____
_____
_____
_____
_____
_____
_____

Un Stress!

Too Blessed to be stressed
As many of you have said.

With God in your heart
No need for stress in your head.

Although you may get tripped
Or blocked in your way.

Maybe you are not close enough
To God, to hear Him say.

How He will provide All needs
At His given time,

Your wants are instant,
Causing stress in your mind.

So undress the stress,
talk to Him, move near,

Guaranteed you will not go wrong,
You are in the best hands, His Care!

Un Stress!_____

_____
_____
_____
_____
_____
_____
_____
_____
_____
_____
_____
_____
_____
_____
_____
_____
_____
_____
_____
_____
_____
_____
_____
_____
_____
_____
_____
_____
_____
_____
_____
_____
_____
_____
_____
_____
_____

Keep Lifting

When you lifted me once,
I was able to see under

When you lifted me twice,
Those around began to wonder.

Three times was too much
Many questions asked

Ridiculously a fourth,
However long this will last.

I get higher and higher
Whether you move me just a bit,

God, I appreciate you instilling
Into my life, to give me such a lift.

Keep Lifting

Direct Me

See, at times I may place
my left then my right.

Into an obstacle of a matter
feeling blind through my sight.

God, I ask whichever way I go
direct me with your touch.

I was able to get this far
because you love me so much.

As I continue my journey
guide my course the right way.

Direct Me! Direct Me!
through another Blessed Day!

Direct Me! _____

_____
_____
_____
_____
_____
_____
_____
_____
_____
_____
_____
_____
_____
_____
_____
_____
_____
_____
_____
_____
_____
_____
_____
_____
_____
_____
_____
_____
_____
_____
_____
_____
_____
_____

Back It On Up!

Ya Better Back It On Up!
Mr. Devil Man

Ya! Better Back It On Up!
I'm in the care of God's hands

Leave me alone
Because you won't get over

Come near me
You will feel much colder

See, I am Blessed by Thee Best
Get it in your hot head

Ya! Better Back It On Up!
As I already said.

It's so funny how you thought
You had, had me

Get a whip of this script
You need Grace and Mercy

As I continue
My Journey of Blessings each day

Ya! Better Back It On Up!
And Move Out of My Way!

So Back It On Up!

Back It On Up! _____

_____

By God

There was a cloud hanging over me
I could not see into.

A blanket before my eyes,
I was unable to vision through.

I tried my best to keep focused
Placing my hands out to feel around.

Confused locked and trapped, in a maze
I automatically kneeled to the ground.

I toned my voice for moments
Realizing all would gradually clear.

I was able to raise my head and get back up
Because God was truly there.

By God _____

_____
_____
_____
_____
_____
_____
_____
_____
_____
_____
_____
_____
_____
_____
_____
_____
_____
_____
_____
_____
_____
_____
_____
_____
_____
_____
_____
_____
_____
_____
_____
_____
_____
_____

So Excited!

Listen Up! Listen Up!
Do you know what God has done for me?

If I just begin to tell you
It would take until eternity.

Each and every day of my life
I am so so Blessed.

I just don't have enough time to explain
And He is not done with me yet.

Oh Wow! Where would I start?
Even if I had the chance.

Ha! And you look at me funny
As I do my dance.

You just don't know or maybe
You don't fully understand,

See, I am Blessed by the Best
Right from the palm of His hands.

No need for me to worry
I just Utter and Pray.

Brought me form where I was at
I am Blessed and on my way.

I Am So Excited!

So Excited! _____

_____
_____
_____
_____
_____
_____
_____
_____
_____
_____
_____
_____
_____
_____
_____
_____
_____
_____
_____
_____
_____
_____
_____
_____
_____
_____
_____
_____
_____
_____
_____
_____
_____
_____
_____
_____

Over Qualified

If God had a resume
What would it say?

I'm sure He would over qualify
For any position displayed.

His work experience listed
On a non-ending log.

Just look at yourself and look around
He's had so many jobs.

Educated to the fullest
He knows everything.

Certified and licensed in any area
You can think.

Career goals would say
He loves unconditionally.

Characteristics there's so much
Filled with Pure Quality.

Not to think His paperwork
Would sit in a pile on someone's desk.

Because once His name is recognized
You will know, He Fits Best!

Over Qualified! _____

_____
_____
_____
_____
_____
_____
_____
_____
_____
_____
_____
_____
_____
_____
_____
_____
_____
_____
_____
_____
_____
_____
_____
_____
_____
_____
_____
_____
_____
_____
_____
_____
_____
_____
_____
_____
_____

I Stumbled!
Through the course of my way
I made a mistake.

My faith was in God
And somehow drifted away.

I would hang where I didn't belong
Negative friends I would keep.

Saved by His Grace
And touched with His Mercy.

A good time I was having
All of what "I" thought I desired.

Until I slipped and fell
To a point He did not admire.

I Stumbled!
I Stumbled!
I Stumbled so hard!
Began to believe Him backwards
Only to realize, No it's God!
What should I do?
Because I know Him to be true.

So I dropped to my knees
And promised to stick to Him like glue.

He picked me right back up
And said, "I forgive you, Now let's go!"

For you, I used as an example
For others, just to show.

Continue to worship My Name
Because I have such purpose for your life.

Always keep me in your heart
And Everything will be right.

So Never will I forget the time
I Stumbled!, I Stumbled!
I Stumbled So Hard!

Began to believe Him backwards
Only to realize, No It's God!

I Stumbled! _____

_____
_____
_____
_____
_____
_____
_____
_____
_____
_____
_____
_____
_____
_____
_____
_____
_____
_____
_____
_____
_____
_____
_____
_____
_____
_____
_____
_____
_____
_____
_____
_____
_____
_____
_____
_____
_____
_____
_____

A Prayer To You
I said a Prayer for you today
To put in your sack.
Please say one for me
Cause I would like one back.

I Pray for your safety
As you leave your home.
Where ever you are, He will never
Leave you alone.

I Pray there is food on your table
For your family.
Keep your faith in God and always believe.

I Pray that you operate
Through His purpose for you,
Challenges and struggles will come
However, He will see you through.

I Pray for every thought
You may doubt in your mind.
He may not come when you want to,
Trust He is always on time.

I Pray you are not ashamed
to shed those tears.
Just count your Blessing of how many years?

I Pray when your ill
He heals to make things right.
Whether it's wee hours in the morn
Or late at night.

I Pray that you understand
He loves you unconditionally.
Just accept Him, He is yours,
No Charge! No Fee!

A Prayer To You! _____

_____
_____
_____
_____
_____
_____
_____
_____
_____
_____
_____
_____
_____
_____
_____
_____
_____
_____
_____
_____
_____
_____
_____
_____
_____
_____
_____
_____
_____
_____
_____
_____
_____
_____
_____
_____
_____
_____

Stop Drop and Flow!

Stop Drop and Flow
Praise Him at All times.

Stop Drop and Flow
Let everything out of your mind.

Stop Drop and Flow
To Give Thanks for each breath.

Stop Drop and Flow
He is the only one who can correct.

Stop Drop and Flow
For each challenge you may face.

Stop Drop and Flow
To encourage your faith.

Stop Drop and Flow
And worship His Holy Name.

Stop Drop and Flow
Never ever be ashamed.

Stop Drop and Flow
Throughout your entire household.

Stop Drop and Flow
Have you noticed, you are on a roll?

Stop Drop and Flow
Continue to worship God and be Blessed.

Stop Drop and Flow
Cause He is not done with you yet!

Stop Drop and Flow! _____

_____
_____
_____
_____
_____
_____
_____
_____
_____
_____
_____
_____
_____
_____
_____
_____
_____
_____
_____
_____
_____
_____
_____
_____
_____
_____
_____
_____
_____
_____
_____
_____
_____
_____
_____

Celebrating God

I am Celebrating God
Because He is in the house.

Whatever He brings me into,
He will definitely see me out.

I am Celebrating God
Because He is in the building.

Picked me up from the floor,
Lifting me to the highest ceiling.

I am Celebrating God
Because He is so amazing.

Knocked down walls, build up blocks
For whatever, I may be facing.

I am Celebrating God
Because He has a purpose for me.

Allowed doors to open
For plenty opportunities.

I am Celebrating God
There is just no other way.

So many Blessings pouring around me
What more can I say?

Celebrating God! _____

_____
_____
_____
_____
_____
_____
_____
_____
_____
_____
_____
_____
_____
_____
_____
_____
_____
_____
_____
_____
_____
_____
_____
_____
_____
_____
_____
_____
_____
_____
_____
_____
_____
_____
_____
_____

A Touch!

There are sometimes
I need a touch.

Things seem so heavy
It gets too much.

No matter the time
The day remains.

Pulled off to the side
To call His name.

I know
He will never leave me alone.

Just a touch is needed
For I have known.

God is Good
All the time.

Just a touch from Him
And things are fine.

I will not give in
To tamper my purpose

A touch from God
Is Oh so worth it!

A Touch! _____

Just A Product

Talk about me,
I am a product of God.

I see why you stare,
Because He has done a great job.

All that I am,
With His purpose for me.

I just Praise and Obey,
And He fills abundantly.

So no matter how low you may whisper,
There is just so much to say.

I don't mean to brag but hear me out,
There is just no other way.

When I think of All His Goodness,
And what He has done.

Still breathing and believing,
Place my faith in Him, the Only One!

Therefore, when you speak about thee,
Say this and fully repeat.

God is able and He will do the same for you,
As He has done for me.

Just A Product! _____

_____
_____
_____
_____
_____
_____
_____
_____
_____
_____
_____
_____
_____
_____
_____
_____
_____
_____
_____
_____
_____
_____
_____
_____
_____
_____
_____
_____
_____
_____
_____
_____
_____
_____
_____
_____
_____

Always!

I had God on my mind
Almost ran that red light.

I had God on my mind
Almost hit that kitten in my sight.

I had God on my mind
Almost fell out of the bed.

I had God on my mind
Almost didn't hear what was said?

I had God on my mind
Almost did not pass the test.

I had God on my mind
Almost was not my best.

I had God on my mind
Didn't have enough money to pay.

I had God on my mind
Almost didn't make it through the day.

These are some things, Almost can bind
Because God is so Awesome,
Your Almost is Always On Time!

Always _____

_____
_____
_____
_____
_____
_____
_____
_____
_____
_____
_____
_____
_____
_____
_____
_____
_____
_____
_____
_____
_____
_____
_____
_____
_____
_____
_____
_____
_____
_____
_____
_____
_____
_____
_____
_____
_____
_____

Gee!

Good Grateful Glory,

Gathering God's Goodness,

Gained.

Get Gifts Given,

God Gives Good Grain.

Gracious Garnished God,

Glazed Gold Glow.

God's Grand Garden,

Garmented Gear,

Get Glad,

Go!

Gee! _____

_____
_____
_____
_____
_____
_____
_____
_____
_____
_____
_____
_____
_____
_____
_____
_____
_____
_____
_____
_____
_____
_____
_____
_____
_____
_____
_____
_____
_____
_____
_____
_____
_____
_____
_____
_____

Just Not Enough!

Thank You! Thank You!
Are words of my Gratitude

However, it seems as though it's not enough
Almost feeling rude.

I am truly Grateful
Of how long you have kept me.

Whether I deserve it or not,
Touched by your Grace and Mercy.

How I appreciate each and every second,
Allowing me to have life.

Only through you, God
Shall I cooperate for things to be right.

Thank You! Thank You!
Are words of my Gratitude.

Although it still seems it's not much,
Almost feeling rude.

I make sure to Praise you daily,
Because You Bless me constantly.

As I have You in my heart
I certainly worry-free.

There is no price I could ever pay for
What you provide.

So emotionally I may get,
Too much to hold inside.

Thank You! Thank You!
Are words of my gratitude.

However it seems as though, it's not enough
Feeling almost rude.

Just Not Enough! _____

_____
_____
_____
_____
_____
_____
_____
_____
_____
_____
_____
_____
_____
_____
_____
_____
_____
_____
_____
_____
_____
_____
_____
_____
_____
_____
_____
_____
_____
_____
_____
_____
_____
_____
_____

Praying Tears

As I begin to think of how
I have been kept so whole.

A puddle streams up
From the depths of my soul.

My mind say things
My lips don't blare

Because of His Goodness and Mercy
That's why they appear.

It feels like rain
In my forecast every day.

Soaked to the limit
Seems like no other way.

Showing my appreciation
Drip Drip as they fall

Being able to release them
Is the best gift of all.

Praying Tears!_____

Getting In Touch With God!

I don't need a cell phone to dial
or text to write.

I don't have to worry about any minutes
during the day or at night.

If I send an email
and if the address is correct.

If I Google or Search
some have restricted limits.

If I use a laptop
it may freeze at times.

If it's a home computer,
usually an interruption in the line.

If I pick up the cordless
pure static I hear.

If I use a walkie talkie
it's just so unclear.

If I have to detect with a radar
to seek His location

To use a GPS,
I would need, His information.

Well, If you know the God, I know
the only tool needed for 24 hour contact,

Just open up your mouth,
Call out His name,
And He will definitely
Respond Back!

Getting In Touch With God! _____

_____
_____
_____
_____
_____
_____
_____
_____
_____
_____
_____
_____
_____
_____
_____
_____
_____
_____
_____
_____
_____
_____
_____
_____
_____
_____
_____
_____
_____
_____
_____
_____
_____

Closed Door!

Boom! The door shut close
there was just no way.

A confused mind, in my head
is where everything remained.

I tried to turn the knob
it would not open at all.

I fought and I tried
to kick in the wall.

Pushed into a corner
to patiently await.

At that time
I built up my faith.

As I prayed to God
not even finishing the last word.

I got back up
and turned the knob, as I heard:

Only when it is time my child
I will see you through.

There is nothing in this world
I cannot do.

However, only when I go by
My agenda will you be able to proceed.

Your immediate wants
are not what you need.

So let go of the knob
await patiently.

Trust, My timing is so right,
so pure and so complete!

Closed Door! _____

Sister Brute or Sister Drop!
Sister Diddley Brute
she's just too cute.

When it's time to Praise God
she's brushing her suit.

Wide gold brim hat to match
with her embellished heels.

Pocketbook goes well
clutching it like a shield.

As she stares at her surroundings
not to tamper her attire.

Seated in the front row,
Is it her true desire?

Opposite from her, Is Sister Diddley Drop
who continuously Praise God with a skip and a hop.

Jumping up and down
her do that once sat on her head straight.

A flowered dress on with her slip hanging
Thanking God, while sounding out of shape.

Sweat cuddles her temples
For she is steaming hot.

Are you a Sister Diddley Brute or a Sister Diddley Drop?

Sister Diddley Brute or Sister Diddley Drop? _____

_____
_____
_____
_____
_____
_____
_____
_____
_____
_____
_____
_____
_____
_____
_____
_____
_____
_____
_____
_____
_____
_____
_____
_____
_____
_____
_____
_____
_____
_____
_____
_____

Steps!

One-Two
Here's what to do.

Three-Four
Knees to the floor.

Five-Six
Move those lips.

Seven-Eight
Give God the Highest Praise.

Nine-Ten
There is no end.

Eleven-Twelve
Such a feeling, felt?
Amen!

Steps! _____

_____
_____
_____
_____
_____
_____
_____
_____
_____
_____
_____
_____
_____
_____
_____
_____
_____
_____
_____
_____
_____
_____
_____
_____
_____
_____
_____
_____
_____
_____
_____
_____
_____
_____

Time!

If you have time to talk,
You have time to pray.

If you have time to text,
You have time to Thank Him for another day.

If you have time to email,
You have time to praise His Holy name.

If you have time to fuss,
You have time to lift him up and not be ashamed.

If you have time to shop,
You have time to count all of your Blessings.

If you have time to listen,
You have time to know God is Good,
Continue to spread the message.

Time _____

Dear. Devil,

Ha! Ha! You thought you had me,
You are the one who is fooled.

You see, I roll with God, therefore,
I am cool.

All your many threats
And attempts to destroy,

This permanent smile on my face,
Means you can't steal my joy.

So as I continue to live my life happy
And worry-free,

No, No you better take a step to the side,
Because He Watches Over Me!

Dear. Devil! _____

_____
_____
_____
_____
_____
_____
_____
_____
_____
_____
_____
_____
_____
_____
_____
_____
_____
_____
_____
_____
_____
_____
_____
_____
_____
_____
_____
_____
_____
_____
_____
_____
_____
_____
_____
_____
_____
_____
_____
_____
_____

Just Can't Stop!

I Just Can't Stop
Calling out His name.

The louder I get
Shows I am not ashamed.

I Just Can't Stop
Thinking of all He's done for me.

My many tears keep flowing
Telling my full story.

I Just Can't Stop
Thinking of His loving ways.

When I thought
It was impossible, He allowed another day.

I Just Can't Stop
Singing his name with such Praises.

Through His Mercy and Grace
It's so amazing.

I Just Can't Stop,
Cause I am set.

The more I keep going,
The closer I get.

I Just Can't Stop!

Just Can't Stop! _____

_____
_____
_____
_____
_____
_____
_____
_____
_____
_____
_____
_____
_____
_____
_____
_____
_____
_____
_____
_____
_____
_____
_____
_____
_____
_____
_____
_____
_____
_____
_____
_____
_____
_____
_____
_____
_____

I'm Blessed!

You see, many may want to check out
On the express line
For twenty items or less.

You're tripping,
I am trying to find the longest line
To be truly Blessed.

Cause as I wait and inch up
Each step of the way.

I know my Blessings are coming from God
And they will permanently stay.

For if I rush without placing
My feet in His tracks.

My plans become unplanned
And He will set me back.

Therefore I listen to follow,
When He speaks to cooperate.

Look at me and you can see
How well I do relate.

I'm Blessed!

I'm Blessed! _____

_____
_____
_____
_____
_____
_____
_____
_____
_____
_____
_____
_____
_____
_____
_____
_____
_____
_____
_____
_____
_____
_____
_____
_____
_____
_____
_____
_____
_____
_____
_____
_____
_____

A Dose of O-P!
Why me? Why me?
As we all have moaned.

If you are able to look back,
God sets His tone.

Life with challenges
Are the tests along the way.

The real question is,
How sure is your faith?

Obedience and Patience,
Is what you need.

Unless you have those,
Things will not Godly proceed.

So, whenever you find yourself
Struggling to move.

Just remember a dose of O-P
Will make things smooth.

A Dose of O-P!_____

_____
_____
_____
_____
_____
_____
_____
_____
_____
_____
_____
_____
_____
_____
_____
_____
_____
_____
_____
_____
_____
_____
_____
_____
_____
_____
_____
_____
_____
_____
_____
_____
_____
_____
_____
_____

A Blessed Chance

There was pretty purple gift box
Sitting outside my door.

I picked it up and shook it
As I took it up from the floor.

The bow was so sparkly, a glittering shine,
Right away I thought to myself,
This box is mine!

So I pulled on the bow,
It would not budge.

I went to the other side
And it didn't even nudge.

A knock on the door came,
And it was a friend of mine.

She said such a beautiful box,
What's inside?

I explained my troubles
As I previously tried to open.

So she pulled on one end
And instantly the bow was broken.

I stood back as she continued
To open the box.

So much excitement within her,
She never paused or stopped.

It was then at that time,
I realized to understand.

When you are already Blessed,
There is someone else who needs a chance!

A Blessed Chance! _____

_____
_____
_____
_____
_____
_____
_____
_____
_____
_____
_____
_____
_____
_____
_____
_____
_____
_____
_____
_____
_____
_____
_____
_____
_____
_____
_____
_____
_____
_____
_____
_____
_____
_____
_____
_____

Recess To Be Blessed!
What is all this hype about
During this period of time?

Has it been taken too far
Cluttering up our minds?

Or is it a reminder for us to remember
Who is in charge?

Cause you know how we can get
So into it and less focus on God!

But He will have His way
Regardless, keeping full control.

And if you thought, you was The Man or Woman
Sorry to flush your soul.

Re means to do over Or again
so here's our other chance.

Cession means to another
So All belongs to God, The Upper Hand.

Just remember before you mention about a recession
Look around, Can you still smile? Take it as a Blessing!

Recess To Be Blessed! _____

What's Inside?
What's that in a can of soda?
When you shake it up, open, and it burst outside.

What's in a stick of dynamite?
Which causes such a Boom? And an explosion arise.

What's in a kettle of boiling water?
To make the sound whistle, clear as a bird.

What's in a cow? Who moos all day?
Uttering unclear words.

What's in an engine's system?
To keep it running and things going.

What's in the rivers and the oceans?
That keeps the water flowing.

You see, there is something inside each of us
Especially, when we are God's tool!

Follow His directions carefully
And there is no way, you can loose!

What's Inside? _____

_____
_____
_____
_____
_____
_____
_____
_____
_____
_____
_____
_____
_____
_____
_____
_____
_____
_____
_____
_____
_____
_____
_____
_____
_____
_____
_____
_____
_____
_____
_____
_____

"Keeping Faith"

Don't Give Up!

Get Down Instead

Onto Your Knees

As You Bow Your Head

Whatever It Is, Just Ask

In His Time It Will Be Given

It Doesn't Matter How Big Or Small?

He Will Be Delivering

Hold Onto Faith,

With Full Trust In Your Heart

Have Patience And Wait

You're Off To The Right Start

The Best Gift Of All

Is When Your Blessing Is Received

Never Feel Things Are Impossible

Through God, It's Always Achieved.

Keeping Faith! _____

_____

_____

_____

_____

_____

_____

_____

_____

_____

_____

_____

_____

_____

_____

_____

_____

_____

_____

_____

_____

_____

_____

_____

_____

_____

_____

_____

_____

_____

_____

_____

_____

_____

_____

_____

_____

_____

Inside Out!
As I stand in the mirror
There on the other side

Such a wholesome feeling present
That I cannot hide

A smile spread across my face
Because it's hard to believe

These internal Blessings
God has prepared for me

If only I can express in words
This tumbled precious flow

Which makes me want to yell
So everyone will know

Within I hold on logging
Into my inner journal

Now, I stand in the mirror to realize
My Blessings are also external.

Inside Out!_____

_____

_____

_____

_____

_____

_____

_____

_____

_____

_____

_____

_____

_____

_____

_____

_____

_____

_____

_____

_____

_____

_____

_____

_____

_____

_____

_____

_____

_____

_____

_____

_____

_____

_____

_____

_____

_____

_____

Dear. God,
Please put in
Your best in me

To live my life
With quality

Through your Grace
Allow me a better way

With all your Mercy
Clear up my mistakes

I came to you before
And I am back again

Continue to guide
Until the very end

With you who watches over
I feel powerful and strong

Everything is right
And so with you I belong

Challenges I will face
And possibilities will seem hard

Having Faith in You and patience too
As I Pray, Dear God!

Dear. God, _____

_____
_____
_____
_____
_____
_____
_____
_____
_____
_____
_____
_____
_____
_____
_____
_____
_____
_____
_____
_____
_____
_____
_____
_____
_____
_____
_____
_____
_____
_____
_____
_____
_____
_____
_____
_____
_____
_____
_____

Feel It!

Fresh off my skillet
I know you can feel it

Just how grateful I am
To be a part of His plan

Because God only knows
What's best for me

Help keeps order
To support my priorities

However, I have to do my part
And keep my faith

A task to follow
A direction to take

Left or right
I find myself sometimes in between

No appointment required
For His shoulder I lean

To guide me along
A safe clear path

"Tock" ticked off the clock
No matter slow or fast

I'm safe with His presence
Full of spirit

Such a way to go
I wish you could feel it!

Feel It! _____

_____
_____
_____
_____
_____
_____
_____
_____
_____
_____
_____
_____
_____
_____
_____
_____
_____
_____
_____
_____
_____
_____
_____
_____
_____
_____
_____
_____
_____
_____
_____
_____
_____
_____
_____
_____
_____

For Me!

See, I thought it was hard
I was so involved

I took some steps
And everything was not resolved

I sat and thought
As to why such a challenge

However, when things were done
I kept on smiling

My total focus was blurry
And I could not see

I've always heard them say
God knows what's best for me!

For Me! _____

_____
_____
_____
_____
_____
_____
_____
_____
_____
_____
_____
_____
_____
_____
_____
_____
_____
_____
_____
_____
_____
_____
_____
_____
_____
_____
_____
_____
_____
_____
_____
_____
_____
_____
_____
_____

There All The Time!

God knows
How to get me through the day?

No matter how tough I think it is
He always makes a way.

I've even reached to the point
Where I was going to give up.

I tried over and over and over again
Felt like, I was stuck

But just as I thought,
And began to put down my head

God made the impossible,
Possible as He led

Me to understand
Everything will be fine

What's gotten into me?
He was there all of the time!

There All of The Time! _____

_____
_____
_____
_____
_____
_____
_____
_____
_____
_____
_____
_____
_____
_____
_____
_____
_____
_____
_____
_____
_____
_____
_____
_____
_____
_____
_____
_____
_____
_____
_____
_____
_____
_____
_____
_____
_____

_____
_____
_____
_____
_____
_____
_____
_____
_____
_____
_____
_____
_____
_____
_____
_____
_____
_____
_____
_____
_____
_____
_____
_____
_____
_____
_____
_____
_____
_____
_____
_____

Through You!

Through You,
I was put on this earth to teach
And what I have discovered
A closer bond to You, for me to reach.

Through You,
You have guided
my steps to take.
The right words
when the Buds made mistakes.

For I have dripped for them
as I batted my eyes,
Through You,
I would say, Buds give it another try.

Many so unfocused
And their eyes are opened wide.
The balance of life
They face and fail to realize.

Through You,
You have used me as a tool.
God continue to staff me,
In this learning pool.

Encourage and gear me,
Up, full to the top.

For everyday you've made a way,
I just cannot stop!

Through You,
And only, I can fully understand
They ask and I give,
But it's Your lesson plans

So, on a daily, as I enter the building
Through You to Me,
God Bless the Children!

Through You! _____

_____
_____
_____
_____
_____
_____
_____
_____
_____
_____
_____
_____
_____
_____
_____
_____
_____
_____
_____
_____
_____
_____
_____
_____
_____
_____
_____
_____
_____
_____
_____
_____
_____
_____
_____

Falling!

I'm holding on tight
So afraid to let go.

If my hands just slip
Everyone will know.

I try to keep a grip
But I don't think it will last.

Got to think of something quick
I'm slipping real fast.

God, You have kept me
The day before, yesterday, and now this.

Through your Grace and Mercy,
I could never resist.

So as I continue
To call out your name.

Safely, I have fallen
Into your arms once again!

Falling!_____

_____
_____
_____
_____
_____
_____
_____
_____
_____
_____
_____
_____
_____
_____
_____
_____
_____
_____
_____
_____
_____
_____
_____
_____
_____
_____
_____
_____
_____
_____
_____
_____
_____
_____
_____

Complete!

Feels like church everyday
Cause what a Mighty God We Serve.

No, I Won't Complain not at all
I just don't have the nerve.

Cause through His Amazing Grace,
That's why I can cheer.

What a Friend? What a Friend?
Who keeps me so near.

Because His Eye is on This Sparrow
As He watches over me.

I Have Come This Far By Faith,
Blessed Abundantly.

One Day At A Time
And I am kept whole.

As God's desire,
Feeling No Ways Tired,
He completes my soul!

Complete!_____

_____
_____
_____
_____
_____
_____
_____
_____
_____
_____
_____
_____
_____
_____
_____
_____
_____
_____
_____
_____
_____
_____
_____
_____
_____
_____
_____
_____
_____
_____
_____
_____
_____
_____

Inner Peace

Here I'm faced with it
Not knowing what to do?

With You in my heart and mind
I know You will see me through.

God, things are so fuzzy
And I am in disarray.

However, I still Thank You,
For, yet another day.

I have my faith to sooth my side
Because you always Bless.

Whenever, I have times like this
In You I fully rest.

So I take this moment greatly
To encourage as I seek.

Externally You have surrounded,
Now I rest in Your Peace!

Inner Peace! _____

_____
_____
_____
_____
_____
_____
_____
_____
_____
_____
_____
_____
_____
_____
_____
_____
_____
_____
_____
_____
_____
_____
_____
_____
_____
_____
_____
_____
_____
_____
_____

Right Time!

Excuse Me! Excuse Me! What time do you have?
Is it the same as God's?

Because if it's not by His time
Things will fall apart.

I see you getting mad a little?
And frustrated for no apparent reason.

Do you understand?
Everything works through God,

Lay on patience,
Hold on, it's just not your season.

Turn your back, Shout a fuss!,
Throw your hands up if you want to

When God clocks in His time,
That's when you will get through.

So come on over here with me
We can wait as a pair

As He pours on His Blessings,
There is No One to compare.

Right Time! _____

_____
_____
_____
_____
_____
_____
_____
_____
_____
_____
_____
_____
_____
_____
_____
_____
_____
_____
_____
_____
_____
_____
_____
_____
_____
_____
_____
_____
_____
_____
_____
_____
_____
_____
_____
_____
_____
_____
_____
_____

Others!

God wants us to do for others,
And take the focus off just ourselves.

There may be some in more of a need,
Who will require our help?

Could you even imagine,
Where we would be had not it been God?

Let out into a challenging zone,
Where things seem so hard.

He could have left us hanging,
To fend on our own.

No, kept by His Grace and Mercy,
Never to leave us alone.

So be Glad, be Grateful,
There is someone on our side

Make sure to do for others,
As for God, He will "Always" provide.

Others!_____

_____

_____

_____

_____

_____

_____

_____

_____

_____

_____

_____

_____

_____

_____

_____

_____

_____

_____

_____

_____

_____

_____

_____

_____

_____

_____

_____

_____

_____

_____

_____

_____

No Mess!
Ahead of time or before,
You breathe.
Ahead of time or before,
You speak.

Ahead of time or before,
You hear.

Ahead of time or before,
You stare.

Ahead of time or before,
You laugh.

Ahead of time
Or before you pass.

That one we don't desire,
Is working to destroy our Blessings.

He fails to know,
Whatever the time, with God,
There is no messing.

No Mess! _____

_____
_____
_____
_____
_____
_____
_____
_____
_____
_____
_____
_____
_____
_____
_____
_____
_____
_____
_____
_____
_____
_____
_____
_____
_____
_____
_____
_____
_____
_____
_____
_____
_____
_____
_____
_____
_____

Thank You Always!
Years ago I
And
A year ago I

Months ago I
And
A month ago I

Weeks ago I
And
A week ago I

Days ago I
And
A day ago I

Yesterday I
And
Hours ago I
And
An hour ago I

Minutes ago I
And
A minute ago I

Seconds ago I
And
A second ago I

Thanked God for keeping me
Each and every day.

Without Him,
I would not be able to see my way.

So I will Endlessly Praise Him,
At all times

Cause no matter where I go?
Thanking Him, is Always on my mind.

Thank You Always!_____

One More!

Ever asked God for something and said
"Please just this one time."

Not even seconds later, for something else
You are repeating the same line.

However, every time you ask,
Through God He makes a way.

Your one time becomes, one more
And now it's another day.

If we ever sit and take,
Full inventory of His Gratefulness.

Placing them in all categories,
Our listings would be a mess.

Realize, God is our provider
With All stocks in His store.

Ready to Bless, when He feels it's right
As we ask for, "One More!"

One More! _____

_____
_____
_____
_____
_____
_____
_____
_____
_____
_____
_____
_____
_____
_____
_____
_____
_____
_____
_____
_____
_____
_____
_____
_____
_____
_____
_____
_____
_____
_____
_____
_____
_____
_____
_____

Ponethetta Ivy Taylor

Without You!

Without You,
What would I be?

Trying to do things myself
Left in a mystery.

Without you,
What would I do?

Left feeling stale inside
And also blue.

Without you,
Where would I go?

Walking around in complete circles
Because I don't know?

Without you,
How will I ever be able to maintain?

My mind so scrambled,
I can't even recall my name.
Without You,
I know one thing,
I would not have been able to share.

Once again, use me as a tool
To let them know, You are here!

Without You! _____

_____
_____
_____
_____
_____
_____
_____
_____
_____
_____
_____
_____
_____
_____
_____
_____
_____
_____
_____
_____
_____
_____
_____
_____
_____
_____
_____
_____
_____
_____
_____
_____
_____
_____

A Journey of Blessings for _____

Daily Log

Today (Date):_____, the Poem
_____,

On Page _____

_____

_____

_____

_____

_____

_____

Today (Date):_____, the Poem
_____,

On Page _____

_____

_____

_____

_____

_____

_____

Today (Date):_____, the Poem
_____,

On Page____ _____

_____

_____

_____

_____

_____

Today (Date):_____, the Poem
_____,

On Page _____

_____
_____
_____
_____
_____
_____
_____

Today (Date):_____, the Poem
_____,

On Page _____
_____
_____
_____
_____
_____
_____

Today (Date):_____, the Poem
_____,

On Page _____
_____
_____
_____
_____
_____
_____

Today (Date):_____, the Poem
_____,

On Page _____
_____
_____
_____
_____

_____

_____

_____

Today (Date):_____, the Poem

_____,

On Page _____

_____

_____

_____

_____

_____

_____

Today (Date):_____, the Poem

_____,

On Page _____

_____

_____

_____

_____

_____

_____

Today (Date):_____, the Poem

_____,

On Page _____

_____

_____

_____

_____

_____

Today (Date):_____, the Poem
_____,

On Page _____

_____
_____
_____
_____
_____
_____

Today (Date):_____, the Poem
_____,

On Page _____

_____
_____
_____
_____
_____
_____

Today (Date):_____, the Poem
_____,

On Page _____

_____
_____
_____
_____
_____
_____

Today (Date):_____, the Poem
_____,

On Page _____

_____
_____
_____
_____
_____
_____
_____

Today (Date):_____, the Poem
_____,

On Page _____
_____
_____
_____
_____
_____
_____

Today (Date):_____, the Poem
_____,

On Page _____
_____
_____
_____
_____
_____
_____

Today (Date):_____, the Poem
_____,

On Page _____
_____
_____
_____

_____

_____

_____

Today (Date):_____, the Poem

_____,

On Page_____

_____

_____

_____

_____

_____

_____

Today (Date):_____, the Poem

_____,

On Page_____

_____

_____

_____

_____

_____

_____

Today (Date):_____, the Poem

_____,

On Page_____

_____

_____

_____

_____

_____

_____

Today (Date):_____, the Poem
_____,

On Page _____

_____
_____
_____
_____
_____
_____
_____

Today (Date):_____, the Poem
_____,

On Page _____

_____
_____
_____
_____
_____
_____
_____

Today (Date):_____, the Poem
_____,

On Page _____

_____
_____
_____
_____
_____
_____
_____

Today (Date):_____, the Poem
_____,

On Page _____

_____
_____
_____
_____
_____
_____
_____

Today (Date):_____, the Poem
_____,

On Page _____
_____
_____
_____
_____
_____
_____
_____

Today (Date):_____, the Poem
_____,

On Page _____
_____
_____
_____
_____
_____
_____
_____

Today (Date):_____, the Poem
_____,

On Page _____
_____
_____
_____
_____

_____
_____
_____

Today (Date):_____, the Poem
_____,

On Page _____

_____
_____
_____
_____
_____
_____
_____

Today (Date):_____, the Poem
_____,

On Page _____

_____
_____
_____
_____
_____
_____

Today (Date):_____, the Poem
_____,

On Page _____

_____
_____
_____
_____
_____
_____
_____

Today (Date):_____, the Poem
_____,

On Page _____
_____
_____
_____
_____
_____
_____

Today (Date):_____, the Poem
_____,

On Page _____
_____
_____
_____
_____
_____
_____

Today (Date):_____, the Poem
_____,

On Page _____
_____
_____
_____
_____
_____
_____

Today (Date):_____, the Poem
_____,

On Page _____

_____
_____
_____
_____
_____
_____
_____

Today (Date):_____, the Poem
_____,

On Page _____
_____
_____
_____
_____
_____
_____
_____

Today (Date):_____, the Poem
_____,

On Page _____
_____
_____
_____
_____
_____
_____

Today (Date):_____, the Poem
_____,

On Page _____
_____
_____
_____

_____
_____
_____

Today (Date):_____, the Poem
_____,

On Page _____
_____
_____
_____
_____
_____
_____

Today (Date):_____, the Poem
_____,

On Page _____
_____
_____
_____
_____
_____
_____

Today (Date):_____, the Poem
_____,

On Page _____
_____
_____
_____
_____
_____
_____

Today (Date):_____, the Poem
_____,

On Page _____
_____
_____
_____
_____
_____
_____
_____

Today (Date):_____, the Poem
_____,

On Page _____
_____
_____
_____
_____
_____
_____

Today (Date):_____, the Poem
_____,

On Page _____
_____
_____
_____
_____
_____
_____

Today (Date):_____, the Poem
_____,

On Page _____

_____

_____

_____

_____

_____

_____

_____

Today (Date):_____, the Poem

_____,

On Page _____

_____

_____

_____

_____

_____

_____

Today (Date):_____, the Poem

_____,

On Page _____

_____

_____

_____

_____

_____

_____

Today (Date):_____, the Poem

_____,

On Page _____

_____

_____

_____

_____
_____
_____

Today (Date):_____, the Poem
_____,

On Page _____
_____
_____
_____
_____
_____
_____
_____

Today (Date):_____, the Poem
_____,

On Page _____
_____
_____
_____
_____
_____
_____

Today (Date):_____, the Poem
_____,

On Page _____
_____
_____
_____
_____
_____
_____

Today (Date):_____, the Poem

_____,

On Page _____

_____

_____

_____

_____

_____

_____

Today (Date):_____, the Poem

_____,

On Page _____

_____

_____

_____

_____

_____

_____

Today (Date):_____, the Poem

_____,

On Page _____

_____

_____

_____

_____

_____

_____

Today (Date):_____, the Poem

_____,

On Page _____

_____

_____

_____

_____

_____

_____

_____

Today (Date):_____, the Poem

_____,

On Page _____

_____

_____

_____

_____

_____

_____

Today (Date):_____, the Poem

_____,

On Page _____

_____

_____

_____

_____

_____

Today (Date):_____, the Poem

_____,

On Page _____

_____

_____

_____

_____

_____

_____

Today (Date):_____, the Poem

_____,

On Page _____

_____

_____

_____

_____

_____

_____

Today (Date):_____, the Poem

_____,

On Page _____

_____

_____

_____

_____

_____

_____

Today (Date):_____, the Poem

_____,

On Page _____

_____

_____

_____

_____

_____

_____